My story of Pawleys Island

told through art

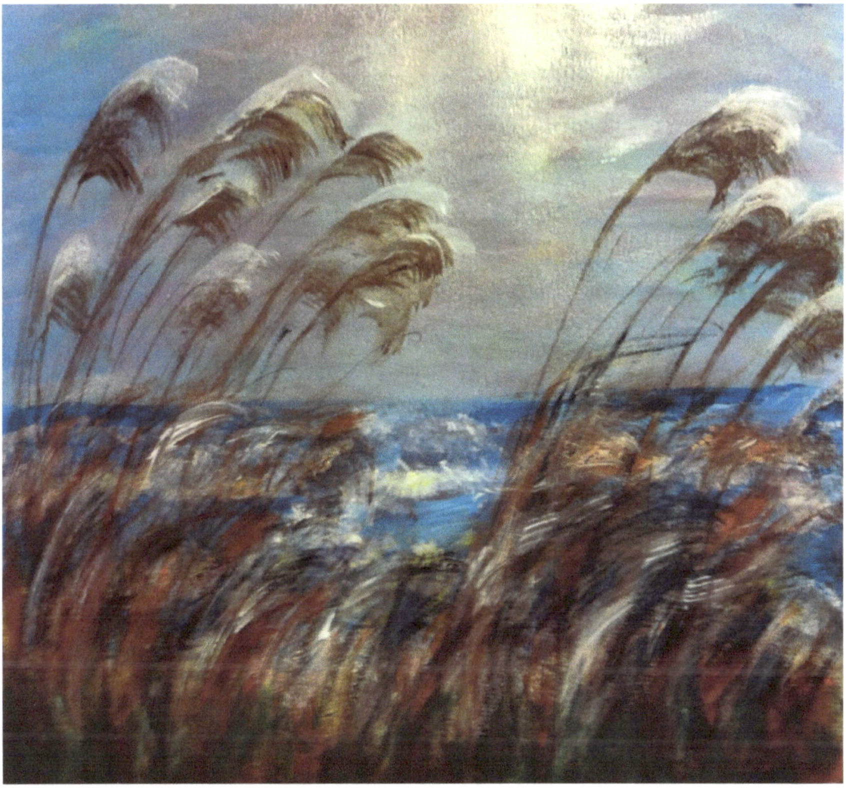

Kay Nelson

ACKNOWLEDGEMENTS

This book could not have been completed without the help of artist Danny McLaughlin. Thank you for your professionalism and patience.

Carol O'Neill is my inspiration for this book. I'm honored she and all the authors of Coastal Author's Network have come into my life.

Thank you to author and photographer, John Kenny for the photo that is displayed on the cover of this book – may the luck of the Irish be with you now and forever more.

Also, thank you to photographers, John Kenny and Vino Paul. Your photography inspired many works of art that appear in this book. Many times over thank you my friends……………..

The town and actual island known as Pawleys doesn't have boardwalks or beachy town trappings. It's slow, private and classy. The people live on island time, a little to the right of bohemian I imagine; relaxed, down to earth, and spiritual. Yes, with the tides, winds, sand, ocean smells and sounds, the soul is soothed.

However, Pawleys can be a frightening place to visit because once you spend time here you can't get the romance of the Lowcountry out of your mind. I know this as a fact because it happened to me. After visiting my friends in Pawleys for one week we bought a home and one year later lived here. Some say there are ghosts and spirits among us. Maybe one of those spirits cast a spell and won't let go.

After moving here I wanted to know everything there was to know about the Lowcountry. I spent months exploring, learning the lore and falling in love. I took classes in art, and it became a passion. I would like to tell my experiences of Pawleys Island through my paintings.

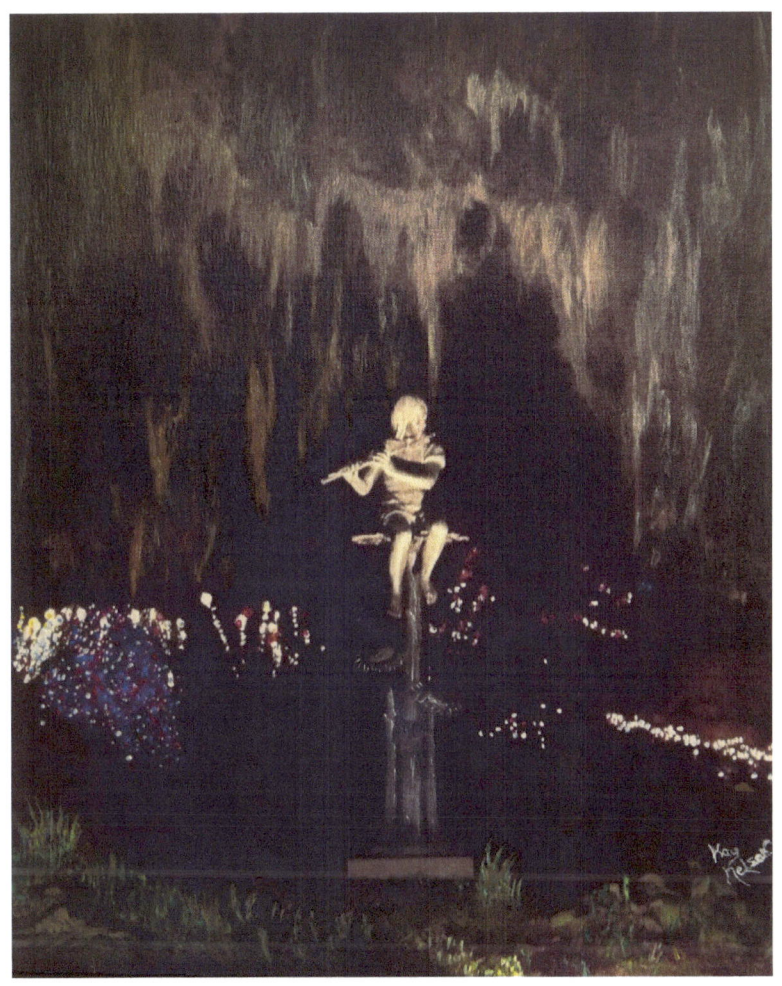

Brookgreen Gardens is one of the wonders of the world, so beautiful, and a relic from the past. I took this picture our first Christmas here. I developed the photo on canvas and then enhanced the image with acrylic paint to add a little mystery and southern charm.

Despite the pull of the tides, or the spell of the ghosts, the move would have been impossible if it didn't have a hook to reel the children and grandchildren to visit each year. Our garage is refashioned with surf board shelves, and eleven hooks for bogy boards (of course each grandchild had to choose their own). The lure worked and the families visit often.

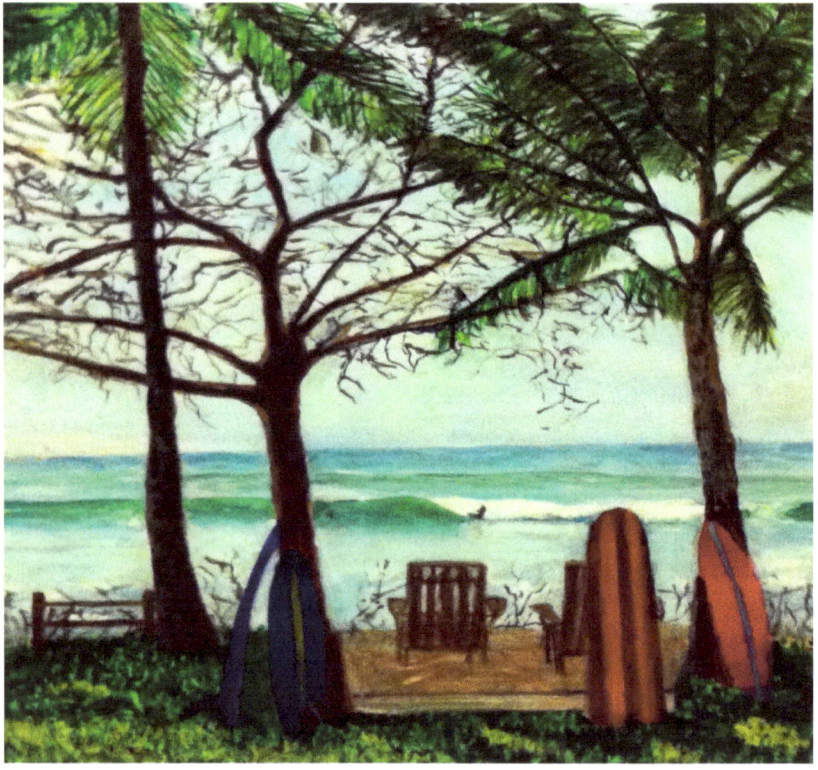

I hoped to capture the smell of the ocean, a leisurely life and surf friendly waves. Pawleys Island is a laid back paradise. I welcome you to bring a book and sit in the sun in one of my chairs.

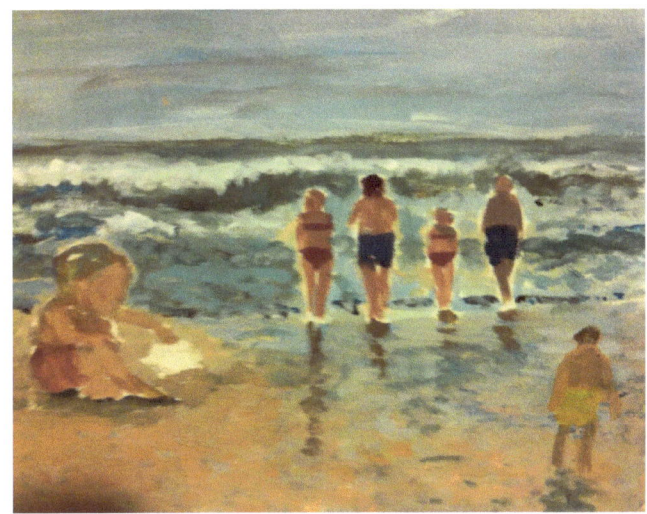

An abstract of the grandkids on the beach. Painted in acrylics.

Of course Pawleys Island has more than waves to entertain you. The grandkids love to go to the docks and crab, or fish. They have an ongoing contest to see who can catch the most crabs. With nets and cages, umbrellas, coolers, chairs and lotion in hand, we make a day of crabbing.

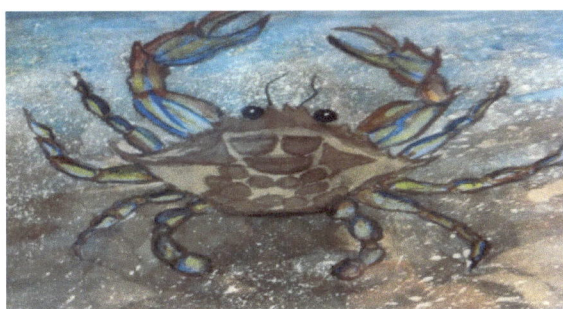This is an 8 X 10 watercolor painting I made for the grandson that caught the most crabs. Every year another grandchild tries to beat the record.

And then, there are the marshes, parks, and wildlife,

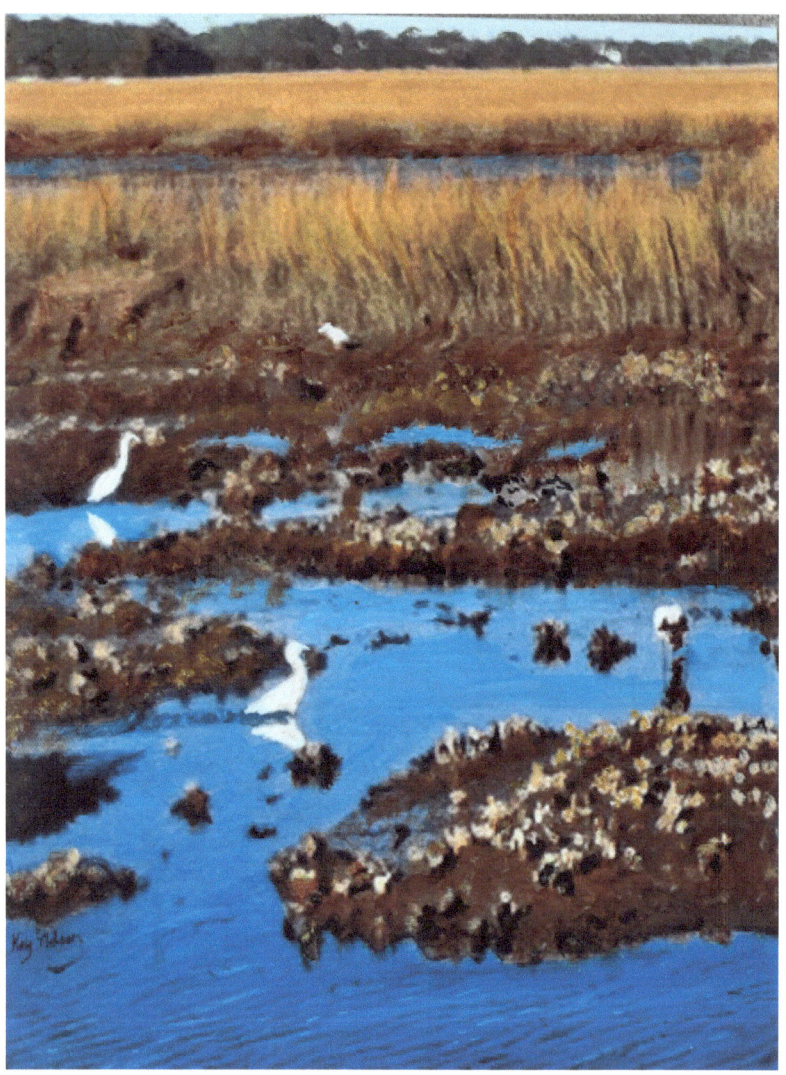

Pluff mud, is a new word in my life. This is also a great area for kayaking.

Went to lunch with the family. My granddaughter said, "Mimi, can I borrow your phone? I want to take a picture of that pirate ship." I looked across the harbor my eyes following her extended finger. The ship she pointed to did look like a pirate ship.

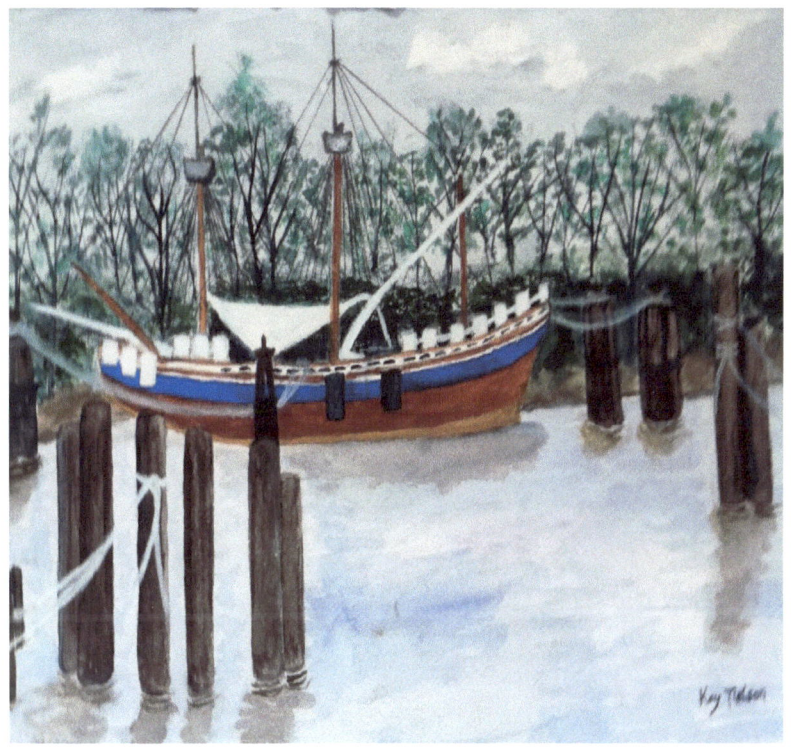

I painted this 12 X 14 watercolor from the photo image my granddaughter took during our lunch outing. Where else could you sit on the wharf, eat shrimp, burgers and fries and see a pirate ship across the waterway?

The wild life is amazing.

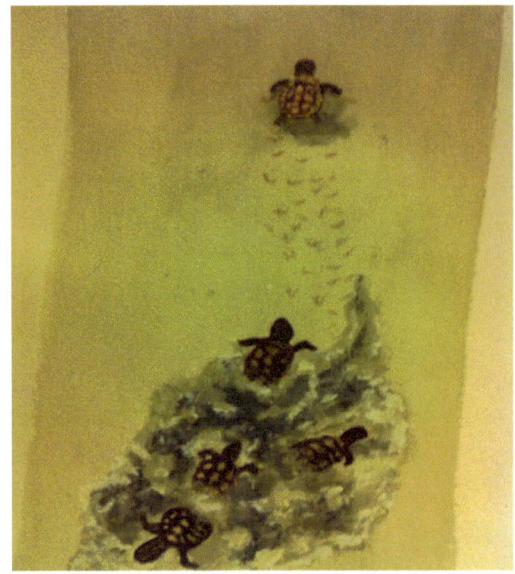

We protect the endangered loggerhead turtles.

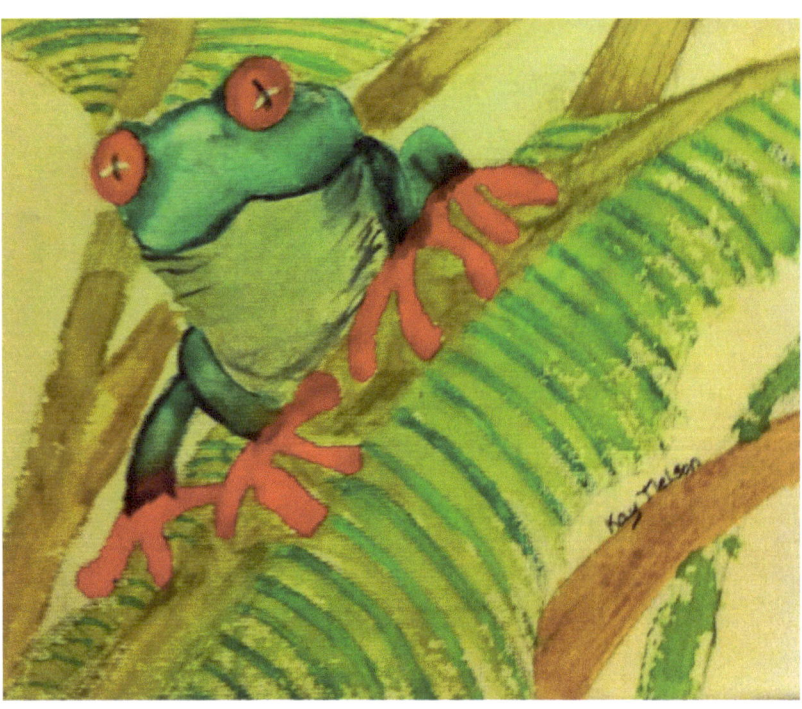

This frog lives in our back yard and makes so much noise...

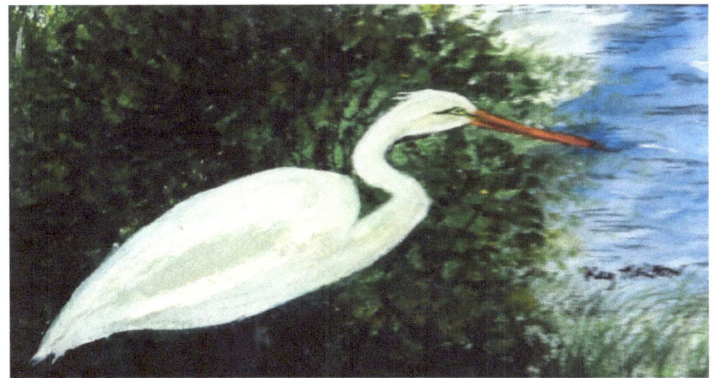

I sent this watercolor painting of a snowy egret to my friend.

.

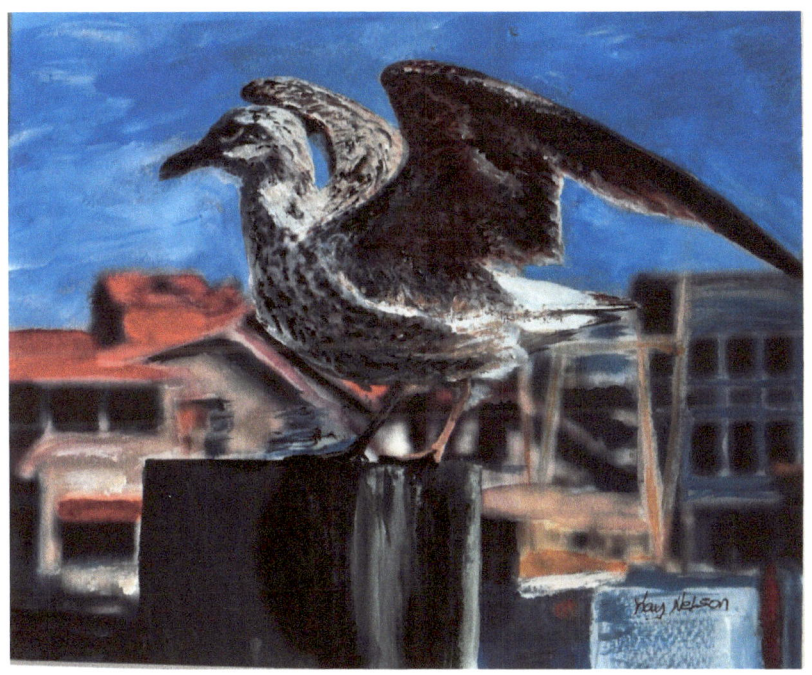

Ready for flight. Acrylic painted of a gull from a photo by Vino Paul.

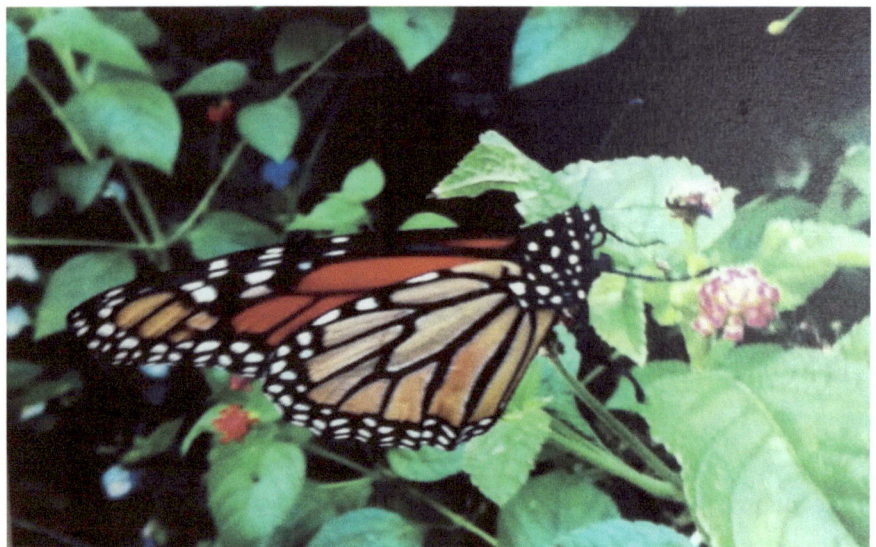

Brookgreen Gardens butterfly exhibit. This is a photo taken by, Craig Nelson of a Monarch. The photo was developed on canvas, and then overlaid with acrylic paint to give highlights and color.

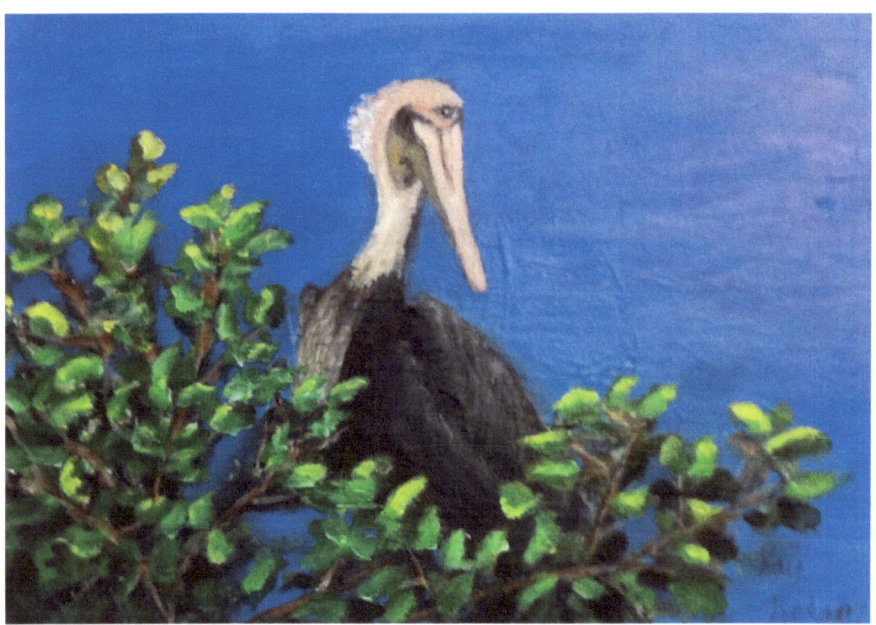

This proud pelican didn't fly away when Vino Paul took his picture. The guide said he must be sick and ready to die. I wanted to immortalize the old bird by putting a little pink in his gray cracked beak, and a glisten in his eye. He's painted on canvas in acrylic paints.

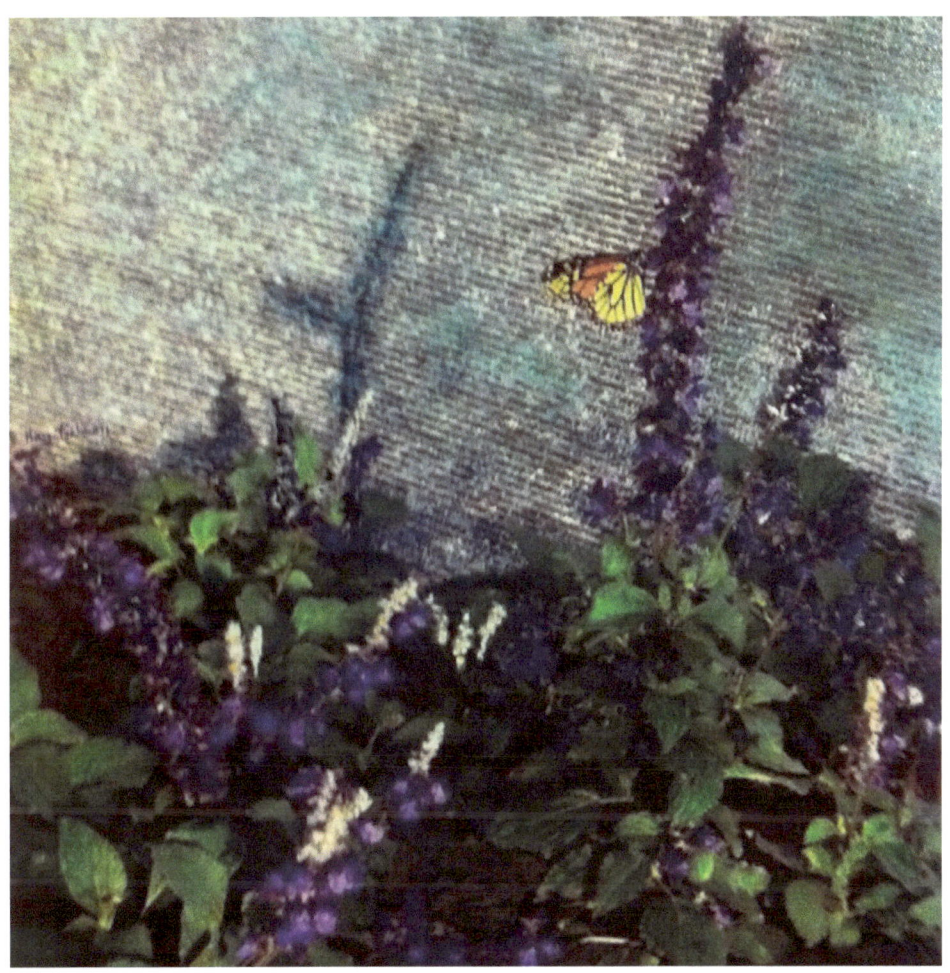

This caged butterfly is playing with his shadow. I developed this photo on canvas and topped the entire image with a thick layer of acrylic paint to add my own feelings and color to the art.

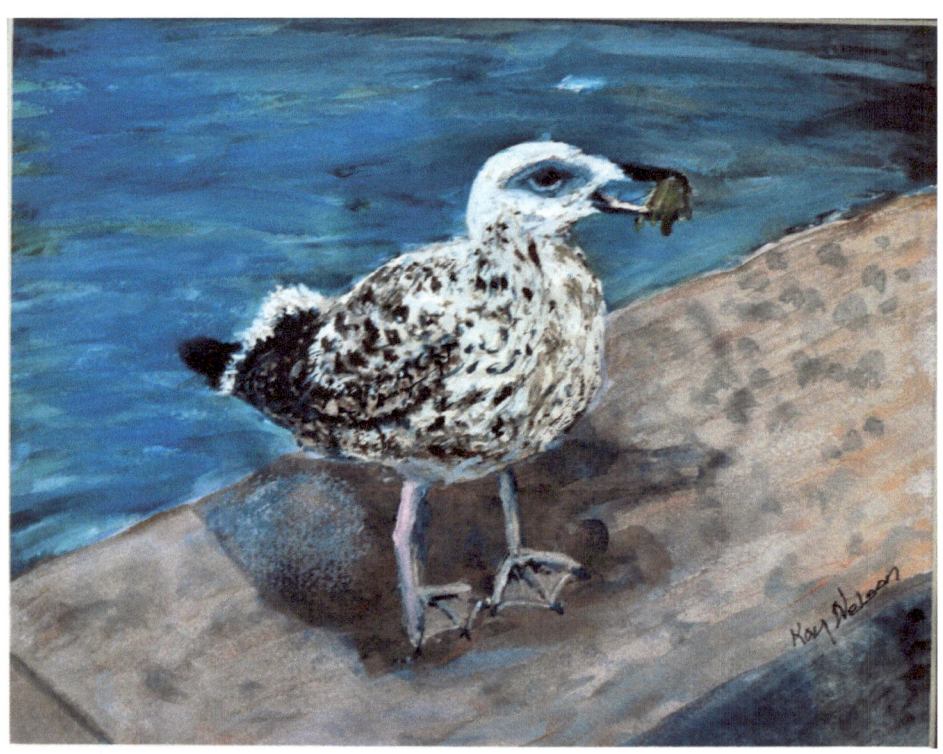

This little sea gull caught his dinner from the ocean. He's a sly one though; he's always on the lookout for food dropped from your table. He loves french fries. Vino Paul took this photo. I painted the critter on canvas in acrylics.

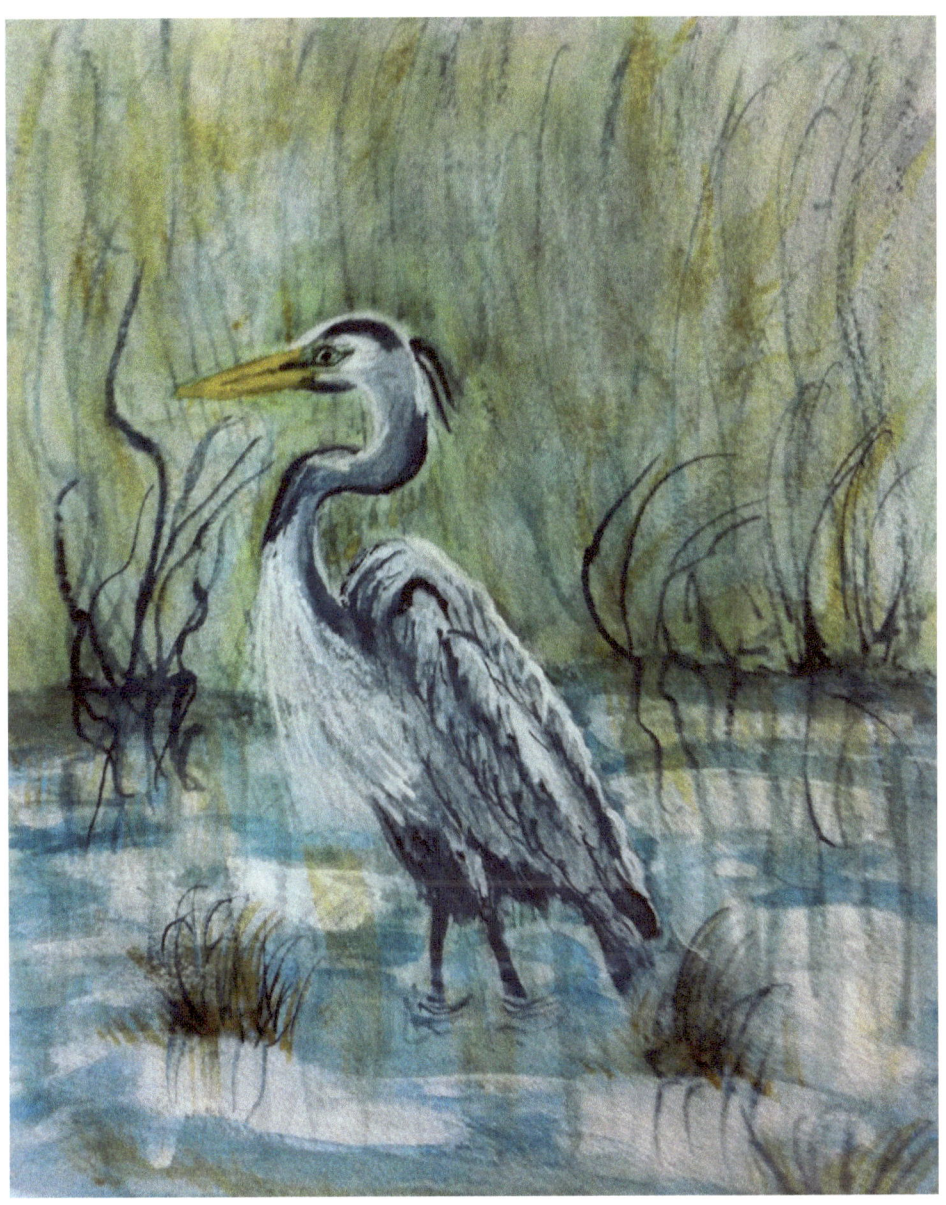

While eating lunch at Caledonia Country Club, I gazed out the window and saw this blue heron strolling in the waters below. I went home and took out my watercolors and tried to recapture his image.

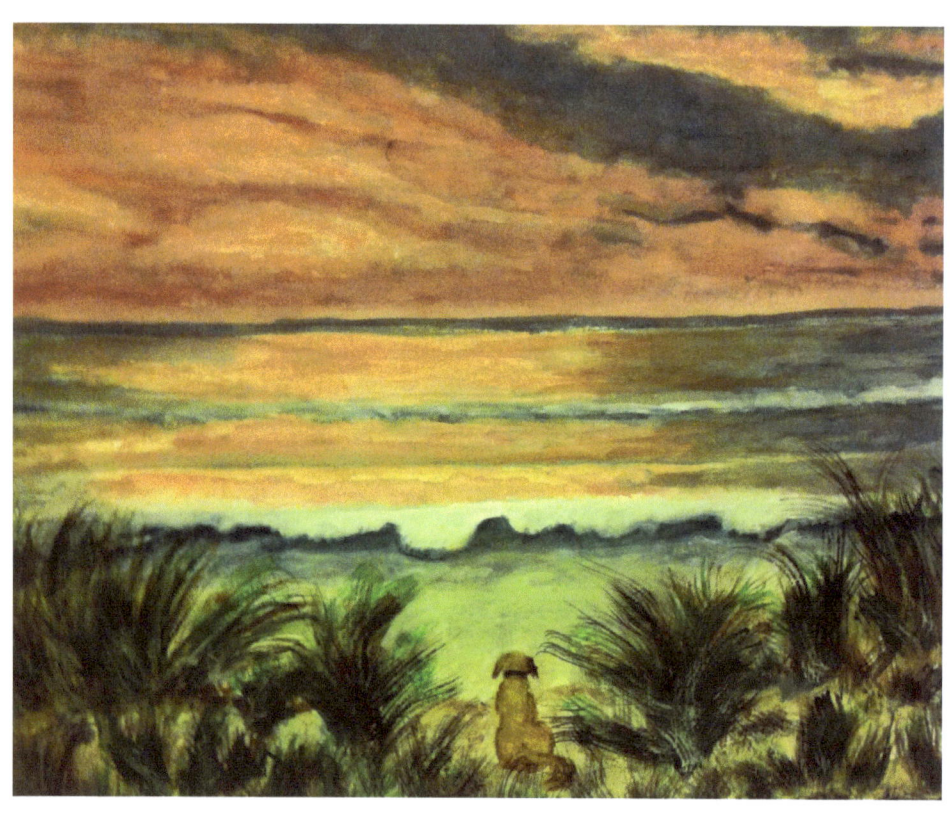

Dogs are only allowed on the beach unleashed early in the morning. This little puppy is caught watching the sun rise. This is a watercolor painting with acrylic highlights.

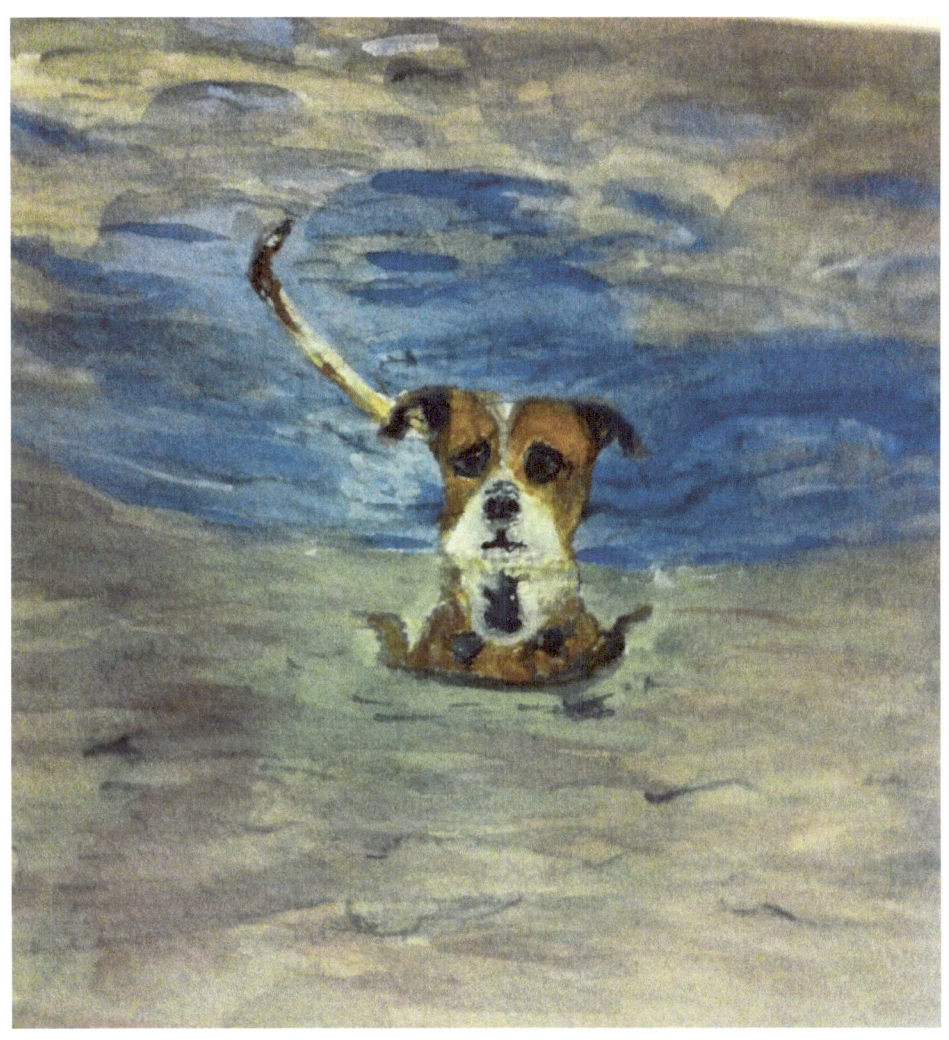

My son's dog Chelsea decided to jump in the marsh. Argh, the pluff mud found its way into our home that day

Watercolor painting

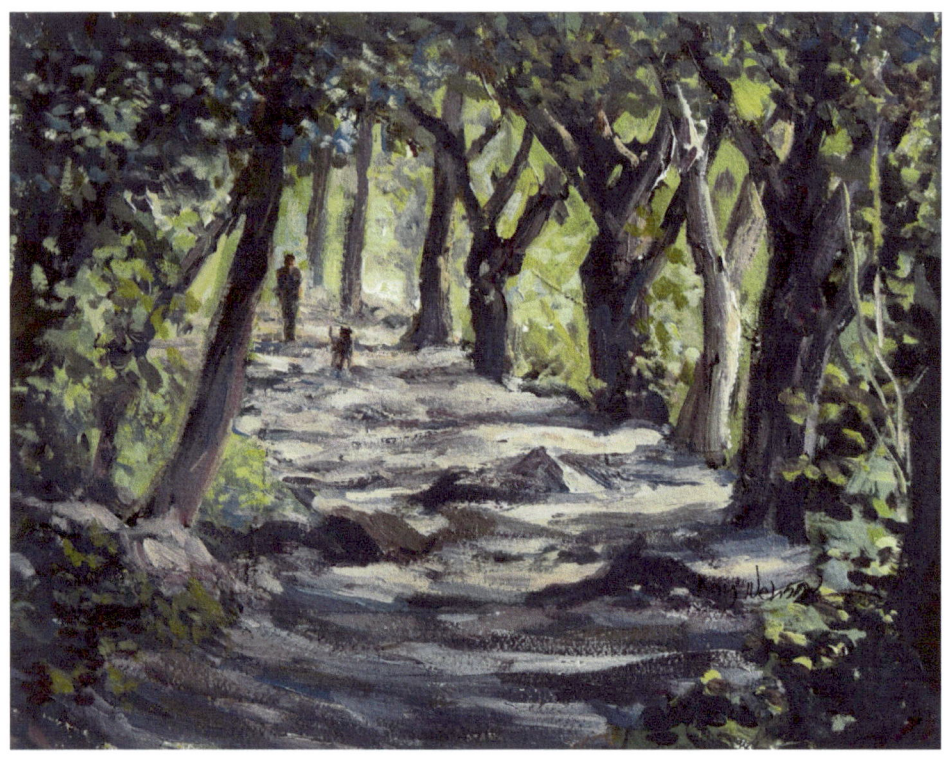

Trails and bike paths are everywhere along the Grand Strand. This one is a little too rough for a golf cart. Acrylic painting.

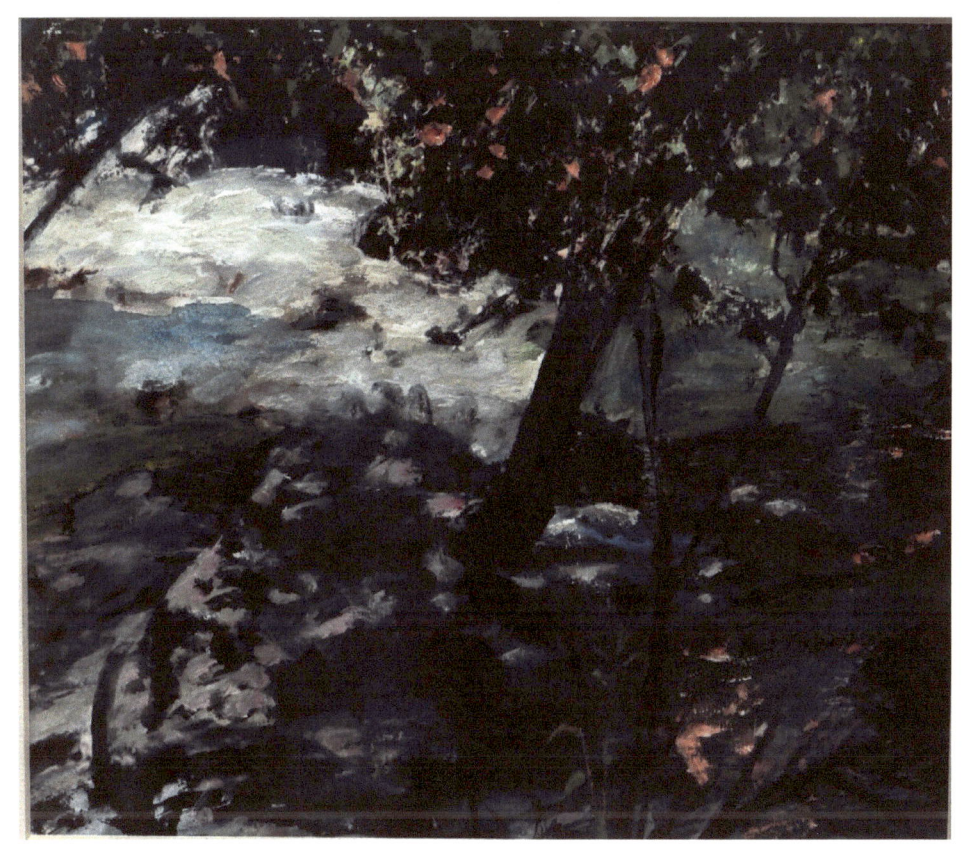

Rivers, streams, ponds and golf water hazards run through most subdivisions in Pawleys. Watch out for alligators. I tried to capture shadows in this watercolor painting.

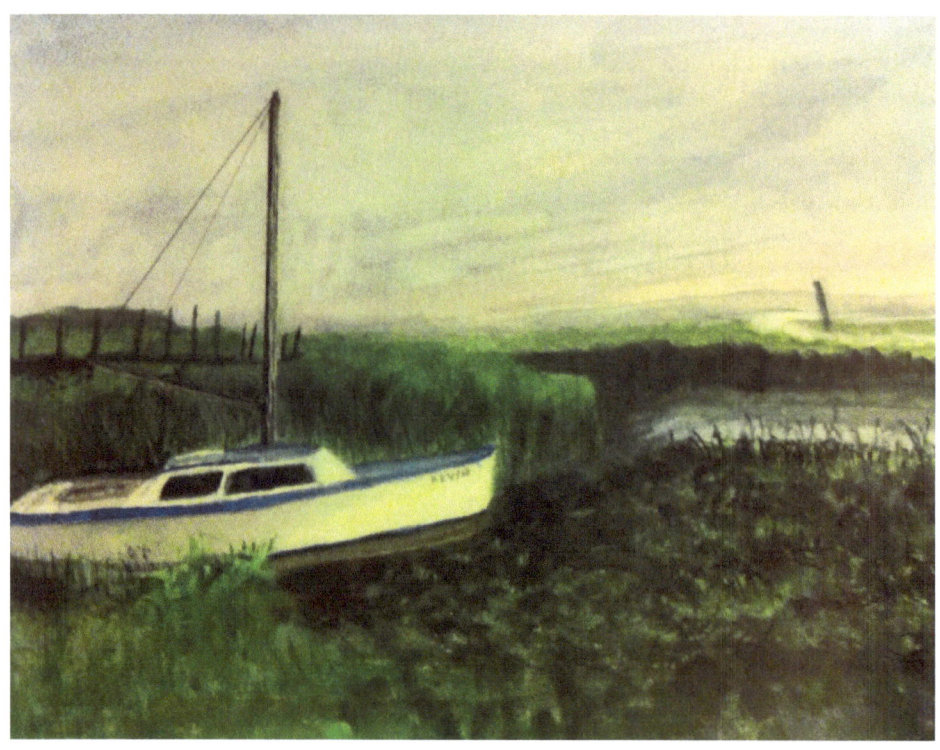

If you're out boating and not familiar with the tide schedules in the marshes of Pawleys Island you just might get stuck in the pluff mud. This sailor is going to be late for dinner.

Painted in acrylics.

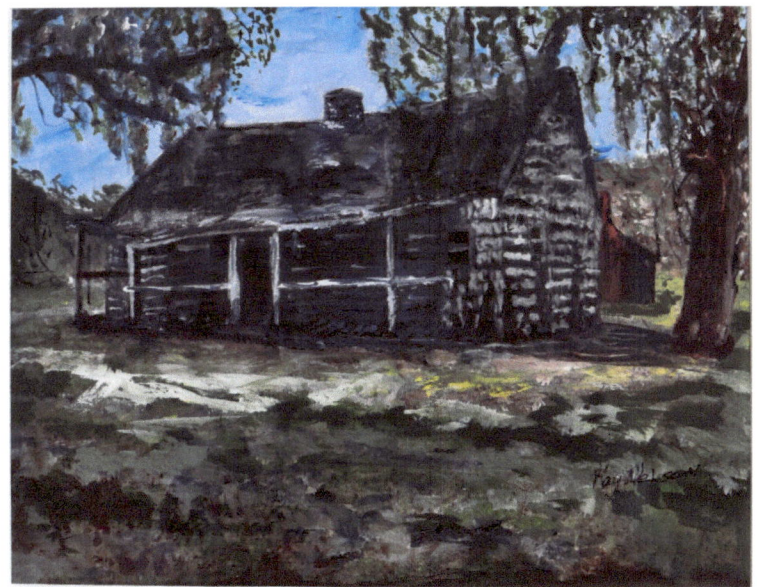

This is an acrylic painting of one of the original slave quarters still featured on a local plantation tour. I've lived here four years and still have only begun to experience the history of the lowcountry.

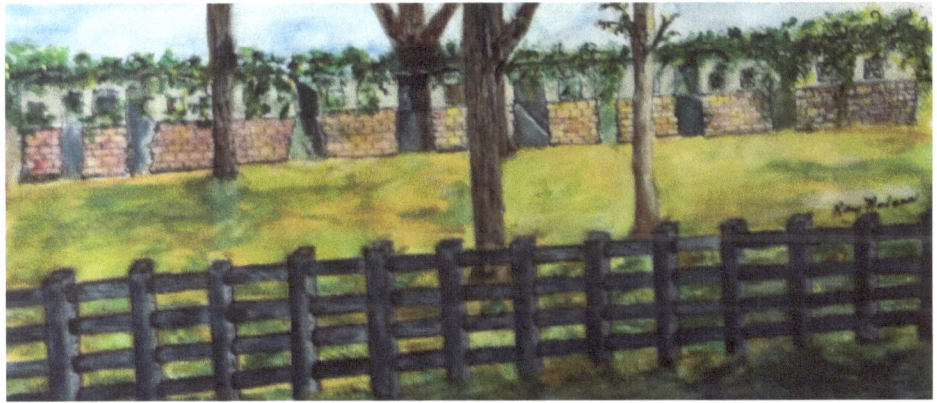

The wall of a dilapidated motel is all that remains of the most popular black beach resort of its time. McKenzie Beach stretches twenty-three acres from the ocean to the highway. Built in 1936 to provide a place where blacks could visit without fear of racial discrimination. Here they were fed and entertained with live music provided by the likes of Count Basie and Duke Ellington.

The more I discovered about the Lowcountry, the more I wanted to know. After reading twenty odd books, historical and lore, taking multiple tours of plantations, and becoming a repeat visitor to the Gullah Museum, a story started to develop in my mind. This is the acrylic painting of the cover of my book before graphics.

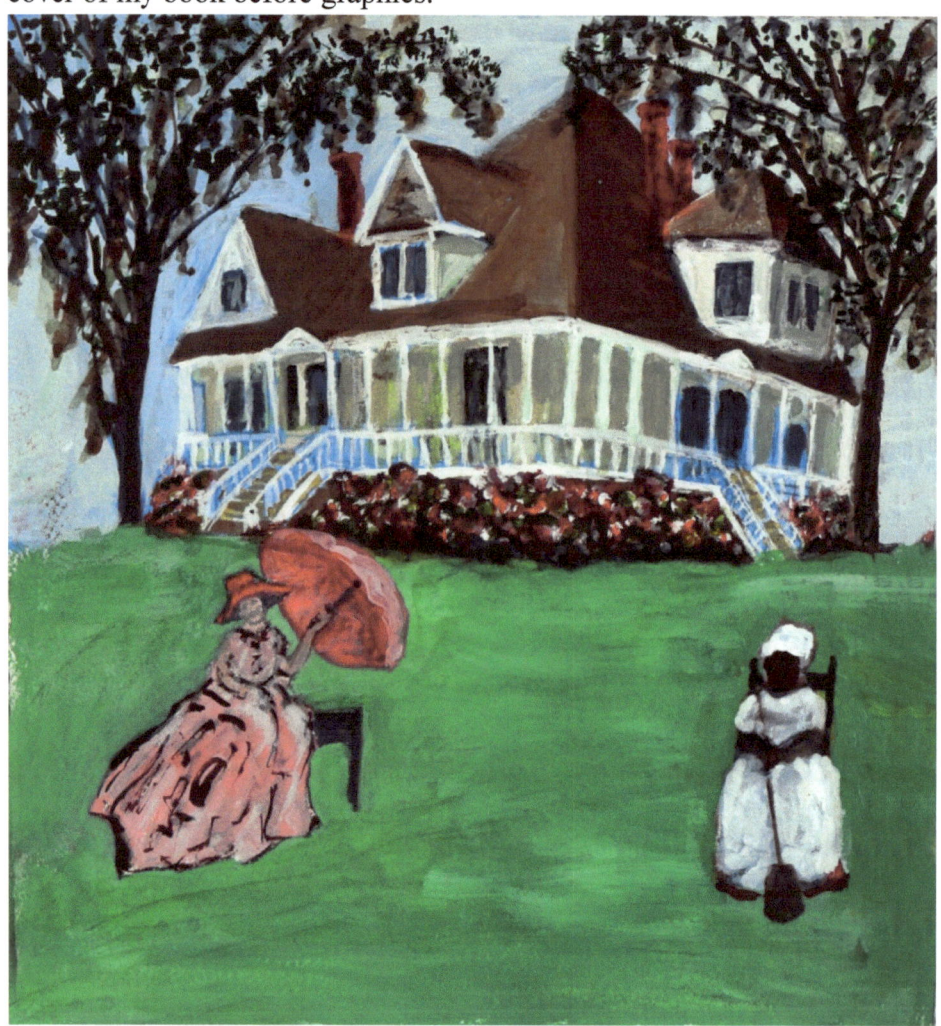

The title of the book is, *Women of the Plantation: The Lowcountry*. I wanted the women of the North and South to tell their stories during this frenzied Civil War era. The brave decisions and courageous actions of these women helped change history. I hope I presented all people, during this tumultuous time, with respect and honor. Paperback is available for purchase on Amazon.com books.

And, everywhere you go there is fabulous food…..

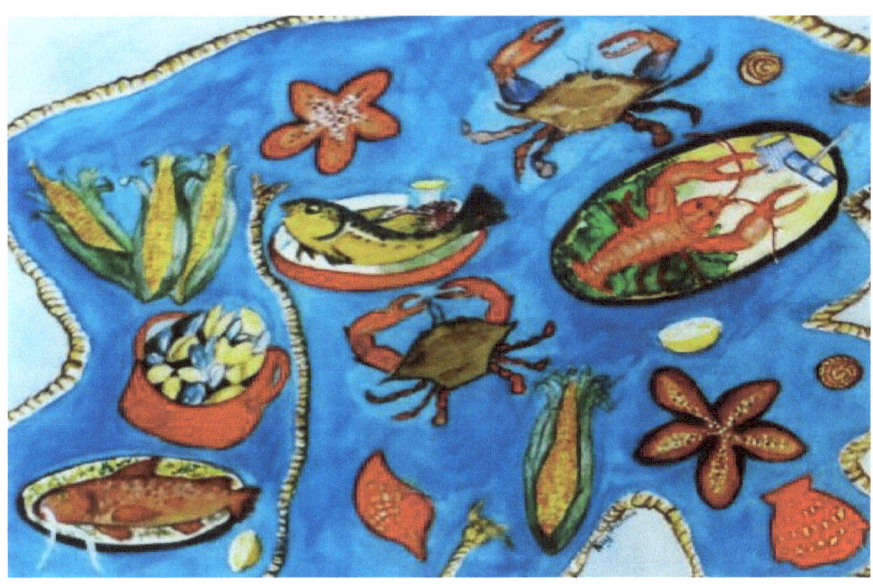

This painting was inspired by a table cover at one of the local restaurants. Painted in acrylics.

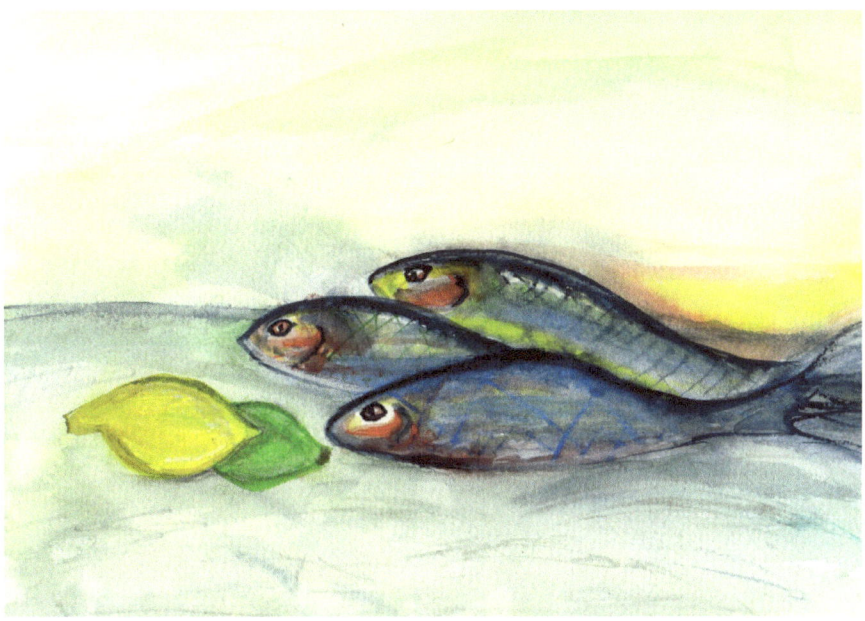

Fine day of fishing, the grill is waiting. Watercolor painting.

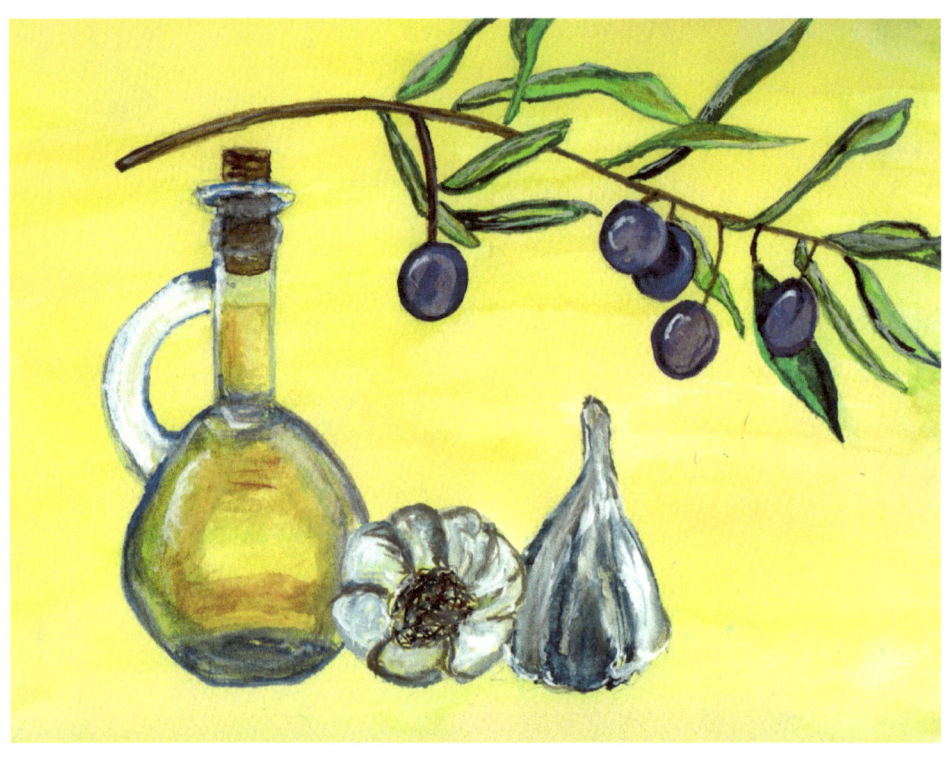

Of course wine and spices add to any meal. Watercolor painting.

The protected wetlands account for two-thirds of our backyard. Foliage grows wild and animals roam free. I adore the fact that people of my town fought off developers to safeguard a great portion of nature's raw beauty.

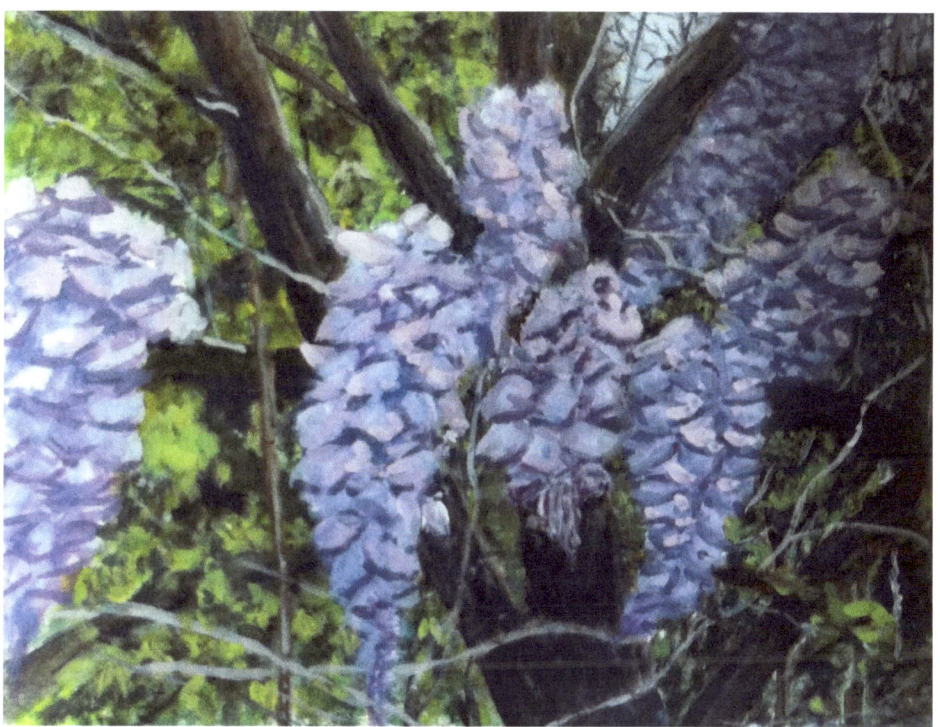

Photographer, John Kenny took a gorgeous picture of wisteria growing in the wetlands. I used his photo to paint this acrylic hoping to capture the beauty of the earth untouched by human design.

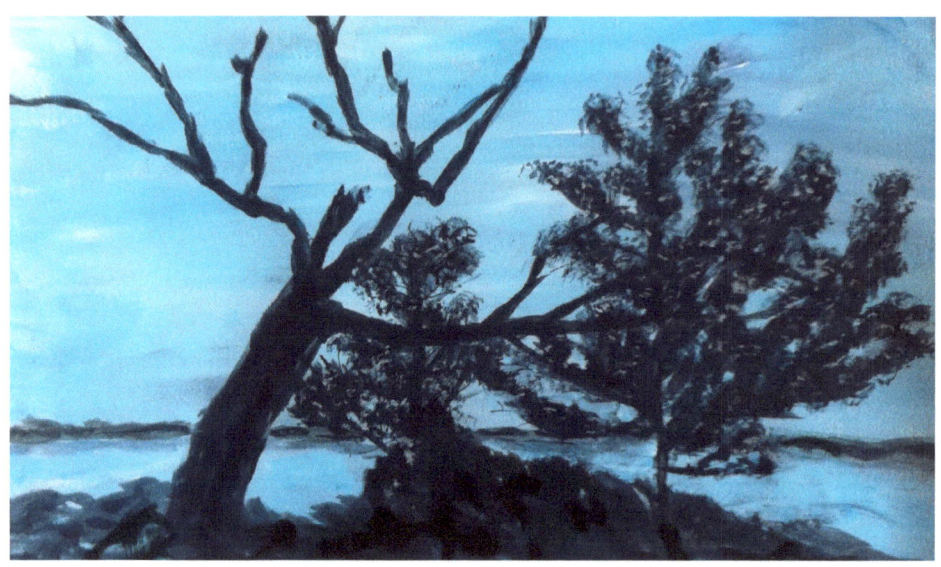

The original photo taken in Georgetown, by John Kenny captured nature at its most primal, fighting for existence in an environment of minimal resources. I hope I captured the story of the will to survive in my acrylic painting.

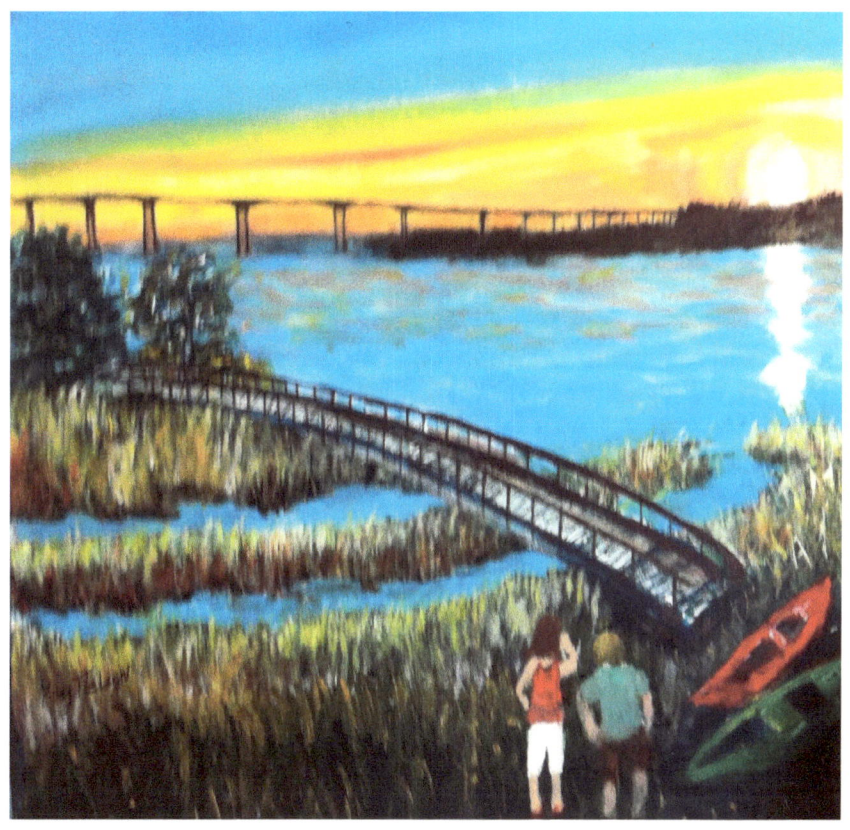

In this acrylic painting I wanted to capture, God's grace. An actual sunset in the Lowcountry certainly reveals God's awe much brighter and leaves you feeling there is a grand plan in the hands of the master.

Oh, yes. And, Pawleys Island has fabulous golf, but that's a story for someone else.

www.ingramcontent.com/pod-product-compliance
Lightning Source LLC
Chambersburg PA
CBHW041617180526
45159CB00002BC/900